T

With love and gratitude
for all you do for me
Lulu Christmas 2002

THE NIGHT OF THE
CHILD

THE NIGHT OF THE
CHILD

Photographs from

THE UPPER ROOM® MUSEUM
NATIVITY COLLECTION

Text by

ROBERT BENSON

Photography by Dean Dixon

UPPER
ROOM BOOKS®
NASHVILLE

No part of this book may be used or reproduced in any manner whatsoever without written
permission except in the case of brief quotations embodied
in critical articles or reviews. For information write:
Upper Room Books, 1908 Grand Avenue
Nashville, TN 37212.
The Upper Room Web Site: http://www.upperroom.org

UPPER ROOM®, UPPER ROOM BOOKS® and design logos
are registered trademarks owned by the Upper Room®, Nashville, Tennessee. All rights reserved.

Scripture quotations designated KJV are from the King James Version of the Bible.
Scripture quotations designated AP are the author's paraphrase.

Photographs from The Upper Room® Museum Nativity Collection
Cover and text designs by Bruce Gore / Gore Studio Inc.
Cover images used by permission of Cheryl Christensen
First printing: 2001

Library of Congress Cataloging-in-Publication
The night of the Child: photographs from the Upper Room Museum Nativity collection/
text by Robert Benson.
   p. cm.
  ISBN 0-8358-0948-X
  1. Jesus Christ—Nativity. 2. Jesus Christ—Nativity—Art I. Benson, R. (Robert), 1952–
II. Upper Room Museum (Nashville, Tenn.)
BT315.3 .N54 2001
232.92—dc21   2001017736

Printed in the United States of America

An Author's Note

What you read on these pages, for better or for worse, is my own reaction to the images upon seeing them for the first time. For reasons that I would like to give some lofty term to, like *artistic integrity* or some such thing, I wanted to see the images on paper just as you are seeing them and then try to let my mind and heart and spirit and imagination wander over them and around them and through them, seeing nothing more than what you see. I wanted it to be that way, and my friends at The Upper Room kindly indulged me. I think that I was right to do so, at least the writer in me thinks that. If I was wrong, there is no one to blame but me.

There is another thing or two that I must say. And I do not know how to say it, other than to say thank you and hope that those two words can be construed as saying much more than they look like they say. And I must say it to George Donigian, Kathryn Kimball, JoAnn Miller, Lynne Deming, Rita Collett, Ezra Earl Jones, Dean Dixon, Bruce Gore, Joel Fotinos, Cindy Dupree, and of course and as always, Ms. Jones of Merigold—all of whom had some part to play in this and played it well. I am grateful to them all. Finally, there is this:

THIS BOOK IS FOR SARAH AND TROY.

Advent 2000

The Story

ACCORDING TO LUKE 2:1–20

AND IT CAME TO PASS *in those days, that there went out a decree from Caesar Augustus, that all the world should be taxed. (And this taxing was first made when Cyrenius was governor of Syria.) And all went to be taxed, every one into his own city. And Joseph also went up from Galilee, out of the city of Nazareth, into Judea, unto the city of David, which is called Bethlehem, (because he was of the house and lineage of David,) to be taxed with Mary his espoused wife, being great with child. And so it was, that, while they were there, the days were accomplished that she should be delivered. And she brought forth her firstborn son, and wrapped him in swaddling clothes, and laid him in a manger; because there was no room for them in the inn.*

And there were in the same country shepherds abiding in the field, keeping watch over their flock by night. And, lo, the angel of the Lord came upon them, and the glory of the Lord shone round about them; and they were sore afraid.

And the angel said unto them, Fear not: for, behold, I bring you good tidings of great joy, which shall be to all people. For unto you is born this day in the city of David a Saviour, which is Christ the Lord. And this shall be a sign unto you; Ye shall find the babe wrapped in swaddling clothes, lying in a manger. And suddenly there was with the angel a multitude of the heavenly host praising God, and saying,

> *Glory to God in the highest,*
> *and on earth peace,*
> *good will toward [all].*

And it came to pass, as the angels were gone away from them into heaven, the shepherds said one to another, Let us now go even unto Bethlehem, and see this thing which is come to pass, which the Lord hath made known unto us. And they came with haste, and found Mary and Joseph, and the babe lying in a manger. And when they had seen it, they made known abroad the saying which was told them concerning this child. And all they that heard it wondered at those things which were told them by the shepherds. But Mary kept all these things, and pondered them in her heart. And the shepherds returned, glorifying and praising God for all the things that they had heard and seen, as it was told unto them. (KJV)

I

The Promise

IN THE BEGINNING WAS THE WORD.

And the Word was with God, and the Word was God. All things were made through him, and without him was not anything made that was made.

All that came to be was alive with his life, and that life is the light of all men and women. The light shines on in the darkness, and the darkness has never overcome it.

There was a man sent from God, a man named John. He himself was not the light; he came to bear witness to the light; he came that all might believe in the light; he came to tell us that the real light that would enlighten us all was even then coming into the world.

The Word, then, was in the world, but the world, even though it owed its very being to him, did not recognize him, and would not receive him. He came to his own home, to his own people, and they would not receive him. But to all who would, he gave the power to become the children of God.

The Word became flesh, and dwelt among us, and we have beheld his glory. And from him we have received grace upon grace upon grace.

In Principio : The Song of Immanuel

THE GOSPEL ACCORDING TO JOHN (AP)

And it came to pass in those days...

THE STORIES that we are told—the ones that we hear in our church school days and study in our Bibles and hear read to us in our lections—the stories that make up the Story of God's relationship with us, often begin with a promise. And as often as not, the promises are hard to understand, even when they are stated with seeming clarity.

Adam and Eve are promised that the garden will be theirs forever. Noah is promised that his family will be saved. Abraham is promised that his children and his children's children and their children too will become God's own people. Moses is promised a Promised Land, somewhere, someday, out beyond the wilderness. When we name the names from the stories to ourselves—Joseph and David and Solomon, Joshua and Ruth and Esther and Ezekiel, for a few—we can begin to recall the promises within the stories.

There are more stories and more promises, of course, more than most of us can recall at a single sitting. But this one promise—the Promise that God will come and live among us—is the most astonishing promise of all. It is the one promise that we want most to believe, and it is the one promise that seems so unbelievable. It is the promise around which all that we believe in has been built, we who have come along these two thousand years later. And it still draws us, still beckons to us from deep within us, still astonishes us, even if we do not choose to admit it.

BEHOLD, *I am about to do something new. Can you not perceive it?*

Those words from the book of the prophet Isaiah are among the words that signal change to God's followers, a change in the way they see and hear God. Those words herald some new thing, some new way of God's being with us. They linger in our ears and on our lips as we enter the season of Advent, the season of waiting, the season of listening to and listening for the Promise to be made and fulfilled once again.

*He shall be called Counselor, Prince of Peace, Almighty God….*The Promise is repeated in our songs and scripture as the calendar moves deeper into the days of waiting, into the days that mirror the long silence of God, the days between the prophets who foretold this Promise and the herald who came out of the wilderness at last, baptizing people and declaring the Promise fulfilled.

We do not hold much with prophets these days. Perhaps there are none, or at least none that we recognize. In the world we live in, there are so many voices and so much talk, and often too much of both, about religion that it

seems we can hardly sort them out, much less tell which of them might be speaking for God. *Assuming that God still speaks to us*, we sometimes say to ourselves, whether or not we want to admit that we have such doubts.

And truthfully prophets can generally only be found out and named after they have gone. A prophet comes and goes, says what she has been given to say, and departs. Everyone was not there to hear her. But word begins to get around, people begin to pass on what was said. Something about it begins to stand up to scrutiny, and it begins to bear the ring of truth, even if that truth is obscure or unsettling or unthinkable.

Why the words of this prophet and not that one? The conventional answer, of course, states that God has willed it so, and that is true. But we who know how stories can be told and then garbled in the retelling, we who know how easily words are misunderstood and misremembered, we who know how words can be shaded to mean one thing and then their opposite on another day, we know how preposterous it is that a single voice, like that of Isaiah for example, can be so clearly heard and remembered and recorded and passed down to us. Yet we believe these words from Isaiah to be true.

We can tell that we believe them because we set out our crèche each year and sit in the darkness keeping watch with our Advent candles each year. We listen to the Promise again and again, and we somehow believe that it will come true again and again.

"I RAGE at my inability to express it all better," wrote Monet to a friend. "You'd need to use both hands and cover hundreds of canvases," said the great painter, speaking for all of us.

All of us, regardless of which language we use to speak or to write, which tradition we have lived in that shapes the way that we see and understand the

story and the Promise, or which medium we use in our attempt to express its meaning to us, all of us fight the same, never-ending, impossible battle: to try and somehow do just that, to make or at least display something that will begin to tell the story to ourselves and to our children and to the others that surround us. The task is, of course, impossible—even with both hands and hundreds of canvases.

And now it is my turn, Theophilus, wrote Luke at the beginning of his Gospel, *to try and give you a full account of what has happened here.* In some ways that is what we are trying to do as well with our songs and our stories, with our books and our art, with our traditions and our rituals. And we are always, in some ways, defeated. The story is too large to tell, too deep a mystery to explain. It is almost too much for us to bear, much less be able to bear witness to it.

But we are bound to try. We have taken the essence of the story—a manger, a mother, a father, a child—and we do our best. We paint it on bowls and plates and canvases. We fashion it out of clay and wood and straw and glass. We sculpt it, mold it, twist it, tap it, whittle it out of something in an attempt to make a reminder for ourselves and a starting point for someone else. A thing of art and of beauty, if we can, something to catch our eye and quicken our heart for a moment, reminding us that this is the season of the Promise and that something new will be born, even in us, if we can only perceive it.

WE ARE TOLD that the tradition of the crèche itself goes back to Saint Francis of Assisi, another of God's chosen ones whose actions and manners, like those of the prophets, were something less than socially acceptable. Those who speak for God are often difficult to listen to.

As the story is told, however, Francis did not merely make a crèche that one might set out on a table or a shelf. He built one that housed animals and lived in it with them for a time, perhaps a little like the "live manger scenes" one sees in church parking lots around Christmas, though it is unlikely that Francis went home to a house in the suburbs each evening after the night's viewing was done. Our way of commemorating his act, our bit of wood and glass and plaster and straw and clay and paper, is pretty tame compared to his. But then we are pretty tame compared to him as well—a sure sign that we are not prophets perhaps. Yet each year we pull our crèche out of the closet and take it out of the box and set it up in some particular place.

Some of the crèches are elaborate, great collections of pieces, enough for all of Bethlehem it seems, with lights in the houses and enough characters to tell the whole story. We spread them out over tables, window seats, and shelves.

Some of the crèches are the work of children, made in some church school class and brought home with great pride by the makers and kept with even more pride by the parents. Each year when such a crèche comes out of the box, the story is told of the day it came home and of our first glimpse of these treasures of cardboard and poster paper, glue and crayon.

Some are the work of artisans whose names we do not know. We found the crèche in a shop somewhere, and of all the ones that we had seen, this one seemed to be the one meant for us. So we took it home and set it out that year and have never looked for another. We wrap it carefully at the end of the season and bring it out with great affection and anticipation each year. It is worn a little bit here and there now, chipped in a place or two, but it is our own reminder that we have waited through this season before, that the Promise was kept and that we await its keeping again.

Some of the crèches have been in our family for years, bought by a parent or grandparent, one of those who first taught us the story. Now it has worked its way down through the years and through the family until it has found a place on our shelf or our table. And one look at it recalls to us in a moment all

Cyrenius was governor of Syria.

those whom we love but no longer see, as the prayer book describes them. We remember Advents past and Christmases long since gone and half forgotten. We remember the way that he read the story aloud each year when we were young or the way that she set the table for Christmas Eve dinner. We remember being all gathered up for midnight mass or the way the snow fell that one magical night as we were leaving the church with hosannas in our ears and joy in our hearts. We are grateful that they believed in the Promise and that they taught us to believe in it as well.

And when we will let them, these cherished bits of glass and wood and paper and straw will speak to us over the days of waiting, reminding us of the Promise that has been made and will be kept, if we will let it.

IN THE BEGINNING, goes the Story, God was indeed with us, walking in the garden, calling out to Adam and to Eve, looking for them. We find it hard to imagine that scene, to ponder it at all—the God of the universe playing hide and seek with us. As the Story continues, we find that God begins to retreat somehow, drawing farther and farther away. Perhaps we pushed God away, perhaps we must do something to bring God back to us, back to the place where we can walk together side by side in the cool of the evening. Perhaps there is nothing we can do. It is a mystery.

As the years pass and the stories come and go, we can see that God has moved, or been placed, farther and farther from us. Even God's own people find it more comfortable to elect themselves a person, Moses, to be the one who speaks to God for them. Perhaps it is safer to protect ourselves from God's presence.

Who among us would be comfortable with a daily walk beside our Maker to talk over our day and to see what is required of us tomorrow? A God who remains at arm's length, or more if we can make it so, may well be more

And all *went to be taxed,*

desirable somehow or at least more tame and more predictable. This other God, the One who can seek us out in the shade, can sidle up next to us suddenly in the midst of our daily round, this God who is with us can be overwhelming. Better, or at least safer, to make symbols and idols and altars and such. We feel it less risky somehow to put God into a temple or some other place and to control God's access to us. It is easier to use certain words to describe the indescribable, and then make sure no one uses other words, rather than run the risk that God will escape somehow and be turned loose among us again.

It turns out that the One who made us is also the One who cannot stand for us to be apart. And that One begins to whisper to the ones who will listen—*I will come again, I will walk among you. Look for me in a child who is to come, born of a maiden.* The ones who hear the whisper and believe it begin to whisper themselves, trying to describe as best they can what they hear and what is to come. They use words like *Messiah, Immanuel, the rod of Jesse,* and *Son of David,* trying to speak of what they know can hardly be said. The collective repeating of the whisper grows in volume until it has become as the sound of a voice crying in the wilderness.

Those who have begun to wait and to watch can indeed do only that: wait and watch. They look for the signs of God among us and wait and hope and wonder if they have somehow misunderstood.

And now we wait along with them again.

every one into his own city.

And Joseph

also went up from Galilee,

WE WAIT because we believe that in remembering this story we come to know a truth about ourselves, that some bit of light that lives within us can only be called forth in this story and its promise, that hidden within this story of a mother and a father and a child may well be hidden the part of us that is the most precious and astonishing.

We wait because it is what we do in the silence that sometimes overcomes us. In the noise and clamor of our lives, there is a silence that lives there unbidden, often unnamed and unacknowledged. And into that silence, some vestige of the voice in the wilderness cries, *Prepare the way of the Lord, and make straight the paths for the One who is to come.* And that somehow if we will let it, that silence may yet be filled with the sound of the heavenly host.

We wait because those who have come before us do, and because those who stand beside us do, and we do not want to be alone or left out. We were taught this story and its meanings by those who loved us, and we believe that our love for them and for others requires that we wait alongside them, along-side those entrusted to us now and that we keep this vigil. We too must tell the story and bear witness to what it means to us.

We wait because we believe that God will keep the Promise. Deep within, when stripped to some semblance of our essence, a part of us believes that this story is indeed the story of God's coming to be among us again. It is the part of us that is the most childlike, the most trusting, and the most real. We cling to it in faith because of our hope that the love we seek can be found.

II

Faith

My SOUL MAGNIFIES THE LORD, AND MY SPIRIT REJOICES.

For so tenderly has God looked upon me, a handmaiden, that from this day forth all generations shall call me blessed. The One Who is mighty has done great things.

The Name of the Lord is holy, with mercy that is sure from generation to generation.

The Lord has cast down the mighty and lifted the lowly, filled the hungry with good things and sent the rich away empty.

The Lord has come to us, and set us free, remembering the Promise of mercy that was made to our mothers and fathers, and to all of the children of the Lord for ever.

Magnificat : Mary's Song

THE GOSPEL ACCORDING TO LUKE (AP)

out of the city of Nazareth,

AS IS THE CASE with a great many of the stories that make up *the* Story, this one is short on a great many details that we would like to have known. Who was this woman, this Mary, anyway? Where did she come from and what was her family like? Was she pretty? Was she short? Was she bright and full of life?

Who was this man, this Joseph? Was he tall and strong, the way that we hope that he was? Was he a local boy or a newcomer to town? Could anyone guess as he was growing up that some extraordinary thing was going to occur in his life?

These details are the sort that make us think that if we knew them then we could better understand what happened and why. They are the sort of details that seem important to us whenever we are trying to figure something out about those around us. They are the sort of details that allow us to explain everyone's behavior to our satisfaction, so that we can put people in their place and perhaps so that we can know our own place as well.

Scholars, of course, can take the few details that are given, transpose those details onto the historical record of the time in which Mary and Joseph lived, and provide a kind of composite picture of what their lives might have been like.

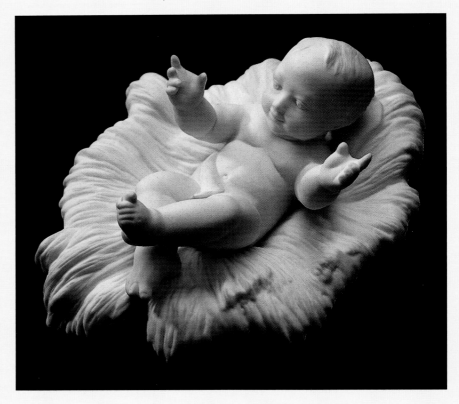

"If you were a carpenter and were Jewish and if you lived in this town at such and such a time, then these things would have been very likely true about you"—that is the sort of thing scholars can help with. Such things can satisfy a certain kind of intellectual curiosity that crops up in all of us from time to time.

Such study and the resulting books provide a rich and valuable set of resources to increase our understanding of the gospel and its meaning and history. But in the end, those things do not really tell us what we want to know.

What we want to know is whether or not Mary and Joseph were like us. Were they really just people? Or more accurately, perhaps, what we really want to know is whether or not we are like them.

BY VIRTUALLY any sort of measurement, Mary and Joseph were two ordinary people—a pair of small-town folks, who probably came equipped with the sort of small-town hopes and dreams that most of us have, whether we live in small towns or in big cities. A good marriage, a home, some children, the comfort of family and friends, a place to belong—such were their aspirations most likely.

They were considerably more ordinary, it seems, than many of the people that God chooses for great roles in the long course of the Story. There are kings and poets and warriors and prophets, people who seem somehow prepared for the great role they are to play. But not so this Mary and Joseph. At least outwardly, they are just two ordinary people, no more and no less.

Joseph had some pretty good credentials, we are told. Matthew traces his lineage back through forty-two generations, all the way back to Abraham. There are some pretty important names in that list—Abraham, Isaac, Jacob, Judah, Jesse, and David. Then there was Solomon, of course, and Jehoshaphat and Uzziah. But the list contains some pretty obscure names too, names that appear in the days following the Babylonian Exile. By the time we have read our way down to Zadok and Achim and Matthan, we are no longer talking about great names of the Story. And to be sure, Matthew's recounting of that genealogy seems to have less to do with giving us Joseph's credentials and a lot more to do with showing us the link between Jesus and David.

If Joseph had some great role within the town in which he lived at the time that he became engaged to Mary, no one seemed to have noticed what it was. In fact, the stories of the birth of Jesus do not even mention the fact that Joseph was a carpenter. That particular information does not even appear until Jesus has begun to teach in the local synagogue and some wag wonders aloud if this young man is not just the carpenter's boy.

to be taxed with Mary his espoused wife,

Indeed, there is some confusion about whether Joseph was from
Bethlehem in the first place or from Nazareth. In one account, he ends up in
Nazareth only after returning from Egypt with his young wife and child. He
chooses Nazareth because he fears what might happen if he returns to his
hometown. Whatever he did and wherever he lived, no one seems to have paid
much attention.

In the hundreds of years that passed between Abraham and this son of
Abraham and in the hundreds of years that have passed since, Joseph remains

a rather obscure man who lived and worked, raised his children and protected his wife in a small town in a small country, without having much of an impact on those around him or upon those who came after him.

Mary too was an obscure person before all of these events took place. She seems to have had relatives who were somebody—a cousin named Elizabeth, whose ancestry went back to Aaron, the brother of Moses. Elizabeth was married to a priest of the Temple, Zechariah. But none of the Gospel accounts mention Mary's parents at all. They had raised a daughter

And so it was, that, while they were there,

who, according to Gabriel, had found great favor with God, but their names are not mentioned. All we know is that they lived in Nazareth and had given permission for their daughter to marry a man named Joseph, who may or may not have been from the same town, who may or may not have been a carpenter before he ended up back in Nazareth with a family to feed and Egyptian stamps on his passport, with a trade to learn so he could provide them with a home, clothes, food, and other care.

Joseph was probably a good man to have found, if a young woman was looking for a husband in a small town in those days—an upright man from a good family, though not, we might surmise, the sort of man who would necessarily amount to much. In the social structure of the day, the priests, the scholars, and the other religious leaders had the most powerful credentials. Nothing indicates that Joseph was any of those things. Still, at least from the little that we are told about him, it is not hard to imagine Mary's parents, relatives, and friends thinking that she had done pretty well for herself.

the days were accomplished that

she should be delivered.

Since Mary was a fine enough young woman to have found favor with God, then she was probably a good woman for Joseph to take as his bride as well. If she was particularly bright or particularly pretty or particularly anything for that matter, anything that would make her a prize, there is no note of it. But it is not too much of a leap to think that the townsfolk were pleased for Joseph.

But by and large, Mary and Joseph were just people, it would seem. They were you and they were me, or at least they were people that we know, if we dare to believe it.

SCRIPTURE gives only a few hints about the essence of this Mary and this Joseph.

"Hail, O favored one," cries the angel in greeting when he comes to Mary to announce the astonishing news that she will be the mother of the Messiah. That is not much of a clue for those of us centuries later who are trying to get our heads and our hearts around the detail and the essence of this woman and this story. One can play word games with a thesaurus and an imagination— *favored* and *blessed* and *chosen, favorite* and *special* and *cherished, selected* and *elected* and *preferred.*

Such clues, if we can call them that, both enlighten and madden. They tell us everything and nothing at the same time. Was Mary favored because she was chosen by God for this extraordinary thing, or was she chosen by God for this extraordinary thing because she was already a special person in some way? We do not, and we cannot, know. We can only know this: She was chosen and that changed everything, for all time and for all people.

As for Joseph, scripture simply tells us that he was a righteous man, which is no simple thing to be, of course, but it is not much of a description for the

And she *brought forth her firstborn son,*

man who will be the earthly father for the God who walks among us. For us, the word *righteous* carries with it the connotation of goodness, of impeccable behavior (or at least socially acceptable behavior), of being a good man. And those things may well have been true of Joseph, most likely they were. But in the scriptures, the word *righteous* carries with it a kind of extra weight, a more primary weight perhaps. It carries with it the notion of faithfulness, of constancy, of devotion.

We find other clues about Mary and Joseph in the course of the story. Joseph, we are told, was spoken to in dreams, and he listened. Mary, we are told, kept things and pondered them in her heart. We can only surmise that there was a bit of the mystic in Joseph and a bit of the contemplative in Mary. We must be careful about assigning the theological and religious words used in our time to two people who lived in another, two people who did not say much about themselves then and cannot speak for themselves now. But the truth is they made choices based on conversations with angels and revelations in dreams that have changed our lives. We ignore that part of the story at the risk of cutting our own sweet selves off from the Mystery that authors the story still.

Finally, we are told, in no uncertain terms, that Mary and Joseph did what was required to fulfill the law, the practices and oblations of their faith when it came to the chief moments in the life of the child. They honored the One who made us by including in the observances and practices of the faithful the One who came among us.

But these are all the clues we have. This is all that we know about this young couple. For all the rest, we can only read scripture and then imagine, we can only gaze into their faces as depicted by the artists who are compelled to draw and paint and sculpt and carve them and only wonder about them. We are left with only our own dreams and imaginings and what we can find about them there to treasure in our hearts.

and wrapped him in swaddling clothes,

SOMETIMES we talk about Mary and Joseph as though they were these larger-than-life characters, which is what they have become, of course. We talk about them, knowing what we believe about them now. Claiming to know the whole story, we sort of transpose that back onto them in the season when our worship, our calendar, and our ritual lead us up to the Night of the Child. We say to ourselves that they must have been extraordinary people for God to have chosen them in such a way. And it may be true. If so, then they were chosen for something within them that only God could see, because outwardly they seem not much different than we. And that is where the rub is, so to speak.

As long as they are larger than life, as long as this Mary and this Joseph are characters destined for greatness from the moment of their birth and everyone around them knows it, then we can easily avoid one of the questions the story asks us to ask ourselves: Could we have said yes the way that they said yes?

THESE TWO PEOPLE, most likely destined to live out their lives in ordinary ways, suddenly become the object of extraordinary attention from the One who made them. An angel comes to visit Mary, telling her news that is frankly preposterous, news she can hardly understand, much less explain to anyone. "How can this be when I am still a maiden?" she asks the angel.

Surely beneath that single question are some more: "What will I tell my fiance and my mother and my father and my rabbi and my girlfriends? What will I say to myself, for that matter? What if I am wrong about what I think that this messenger of God has said to me? What will become of me if word of

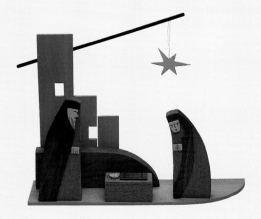

and laid him in a manger;

this gets out—not just word that I am with child but word that I think this child is the One who is to come?"

Word does get out, of course, at least the word that Mary is with child. Among other places that leads us to Joseph, whose first notion is to do what the social order of his day would have called compassionate at best, weak at worst: Divorce her quietly and go on with his life.

Then in a dream an angel comes to Joseph, telling him to follow through with the marriage and relaying news of this extraordinary child's birth, the name they are to call the child, and the work the child is to do. Joseph does the one thing no one would have expected him to do, the one thing no one would have criticized him for not doing it. He embarks on a mysterious journey with this young woman and this child.

Mary goes to tell her cousin the news and, lo and behold, it turns out that the angels have been at work at that house too. Another child is on the way in circumstances that are also a little out of the ordinary. Zechariah has not been able to talk for months, and Elizabeth already knows about the child that Mary is carrying in her womb.

Mary goes home, perhaps only then to discover that after the marriage, the happy couple is to set out for Bethlehem for the census, or so they are given to understand. *So that the scriptures would be fulfilled* is another way to look at it.

THEN TO BETHLEHEM. A long journey made by a recently married couple to a little town to be counted in the census. And what to say to each other on the journey?

How does Joseph begin to tell what he has seen and heard when what he has seen and heard is the news that the One who is to come is traveling with him along the road, in the belly of the young woman who is traveling beside him?

How does Mary say what she has seen and heard when what she has seen and heard is that she has been chosen to be the mother of God with us?

because there was no room for them in the inn.

How could they talk about it? How could they not talk about it? How could they not have talked about their fears and their hopes and their joys and their perplexities?

Yet the mystery is too large to imagine, too enormous to understand. We who have had the benefit of ruminating on it collectively for two thousand years do not fully understand it now, and never will, on this earth anyway. This sort of living with the questions is a way of holding the astonishing truth of it—that God is to live among us—in our heads and our hearts and of being able to bear the thought of it.

But we were not on the road to Bethlehem with a child in our womb, with these dreams and visions in our heads, with this unknown future just ahead of us. For us to believe the story now is difficult enough sometimes, to have believed it then is somehow unthinkable.

BETHLEHEM is upon them, it can be seen there in the distance. The search begins for a place to stay in a crowded city: the mundane tasks of finding shelter and provisions, of checking in with the local folks to find out about this census and where to go and what papers to bring and whom to see to begin.

Their inquiry does not begin well by any measurement except God's. God's sense of timing and humor, as well as God's sense of the dramatic and the astonishing, are on full display here. Elie Wiesel once wrote that "God made humans because he loves a good story." God is not above making the story a little better, we are tempted to add.

There is no place to stay, the inns are full. Makeshift quarters are arranged in a stable behind an inn, hardly an auspicious beginning for a young man and his young bride, especially considering the fact that a child is about to be born,

and not to mention the fact that Mary and Joseph have been told that this is to be the Child.

How long were they there? How many nights did they spend in the dark of that stable, thinking any minute might be the time for the child's birth? How many mornings did they waken somewhat grateful and somewhat disappointed, the way all parents are when they are awaiting the birth of a child? How many times did they say to themselves, and maybe to each other, that perhaps they had gotten it wrong somehow? They could not question Mary's giving birth, but perhaps they had misunderstood the angels and the dreams. Surely God would not come among them here in this place, this humble and dismal place?

We like to think of them as having been sure from the beginning, the way we like to look back on our own journeys of faith and describe ourselves as having been so sure all the way along. We like to remember ourselves as having been certain in each and every moment of God's speaking to us that we knew exactly who was speaking and what the message was. But that's not an accurate remembrance, not really, and we unwisely ignore the possibility that this Mary and this Joseph might have been uncertain as well. Their uncertainty does not mean that their faith was less, it means that their faith was more. It takes no faith to live in unfailing certainty. It takes faith to live in the uncertainty, in the stable in the dark with little more than one's dreams to hold onto.

SUDDENLY, the night is upon them, the way that it always seems to be so sudden when a child is coming into the world. All of the waiting, the days passed in limbo, and then suddenly there is the birth—the pain and the struggle, the astonishment and the wonder, the grittiness and the beauty of it.

shepherds abiding in the field,

It is hard to imagine they were completely alone, though it is possible. The story tells of no others. The others who come—the shepherds and the wise men—come later. At the birth itself there is no one.

Whatever else Joseph may or may not have been—righteous man, member of the household of David, member of the local synagogue, carpenter—he is not likely to have been well-versed in the art of assisting at the birth of a baby. Not too many men would have been in that day and age, not too many men are in this day and age, for that matter.

Did not Joseph in haste summon a midwife, awakened and brought to the stable by a young servant boy from the inn, who had been dispatched running through the city streets to find her and to get her moving, for the time was at hand?

Did not another young servant, a girl perhaps, run back and forth carrying water and cloths, reporting the progress to the others in the inn and reporting back to the women in the stable just how many well-wishers had gathered nearby, praying for the baby and making sure that Joseph was doing just fine?

Was there not a crowd around Joseph, wishing him luck and God's blessing, and above all, a son? Did he tell them what he already knew, what he had already been told by an angel in a dream? Or did he hold his tongue, somewhat afraid of the prospect of explaining what he himself could not quite understand?

Was there not a fire lit so that the midwife could see, and perhaps Joseph himself carrying wood, anxious to find something useful to do at this moment when he was by and large unnecessary to the extraordinary event taking place in the stable? Was the labor long and difficult, leaving this young Mary exhausted and spent? Was she afraid and nearly delirious? Did she cry out to her mother and her Maker and to anyone else within earshot?

keeping watch over their flock by night.

WHAT MUST it have been like in that stable in the first few moments and hours after the birth of the Child?

To hold any newborn baby is to hold the whole world in one's hands for a while and to be overcome with thanksgiving and joy and wonder. But to have been Mary and Joseph, to believe what they believed about this Child and to hold him in their arms is more than most any of us can imagine.

A newborn baby seldom looks as though it can survive, much less become the Savior of the world. Some newborn babies are pretty, but we seldom react by saying that this particular one is God incarnate.

How long before the reality of being parents begins to sink in for the two of them? And what must it have been like to try and wed the ordinary reality of having a child to care for with the knowledge that this Child would carry the weight of the world someday—but only if you could carry your part first?

How do we hold this baby in our arms, look into its tiny face, hold its tiny fingers in our hands, and say to ourselves that this is the Messiah?

ENTER THE SHEPHERDS into the little darkened town and into the stable itself, into the lives of Mary and Joseph and the Child, into the Story and into our own. They have their own tale to tell, but in the beginning we must only wonder what Mary and Joseph might have thought when they arrived.

Mary and Joseph are far away in a town that is not their own, at the very moment of becoming the parents to a child who is somehow also not their own, and into this moment comes a crowd of folks who are running through the night with their hearts on fire and their minds more than a little excited, singing songs and telling stories of angels and falling all over themselves at the sight of the baby in a manger. If Mary and Joseph did not know it before, then they surely know now that this Child will never, in a way, belong to them.

And, lo,

the angel of the Lord came upon them,

With the shepherds' arrival, other people begin proclaiming their own version of the same story and claiming to have been sent by the angels as well. Some believe what Mary and Joseph believe to be true about the Child, others who are filled with joy and wonder at the prospect. There are those who will wander the streets telling all who will listen that the Promise has finally been fulfilled and that all can see for themselves at the stable behind the inn. Others believe that the Promise itself is wrapped in those swaddling clothes.

The shepherds did not seem to be shy about what they believed that they were seeing. And who can blame them? They had seen and heard quite a bit that night, enough for it to be highly unlikely that they just sort of slipped out of town talking quietly among themselves. It is not too hard to imagine them going from place to place along their way home, stopping to tell others the news, telling where the Child could be found.

From there it is not a very long leap at all to imagine others who came, those who heard the news and wanted to see for themselves. Perhaps they came because they believed it, perhaps just in case, perhaps just to be sure that if anything came of it they could say that they had least made the trip over to Bethlehem to check it out for themselves.

How many nameless and untold visitors might Mary and Joseph have had in that stable? How many local scribes and rabbis, how many other young couples, how many other shepherds and innkeepers came by to see this thing that had taken place?

How many walked away wondering to themselves what all the fuss was about—this poor young couple, that little baby, this stable full of mystery and questions and promises and such? How many of us came and saw and walked away?

We do not know the truth of any of these things, of course; we can only imagine, if imagination can ever be considered an only thing. But if it was real,

then it must have been real life; and something like some of these things must have taken place. And if it was not, then it is just a pretty story after all.

THESE TWO PEOPLE are a mystery, even after all this time, maybe especially after all this time.

He is still a mystery to us, this Joseph, as he always has been, perhaps even to those who knew him at the time, and perhaps as all fathers are in some way and always have been. No one of us who is a father is bound to our children in the deep ways of mothers. We are bound to them only by our presence, by our silences and our gestures, by our words and our time and our outstretched hands and open eyes and ears.

It is the silence of Joseph that speaks still, both the silence of the man himself and the silence about him in the story of the Child. It is his place in the story that is most like our own. He is noted but not celebrated. He is unsung and unremarked, as are most of us most of the time most all of our lives.

All of the others have speeches to make: Mary and Elizabeth, Zechariah and Gabriel, Anna and Simeon, even the evil King Herod, the wise men, the shepherds, and the angels. From Joseph we hear not a single word.

Someone somewhere must have talked to him, and he must have said something, for we are told of his dreams. He surely must have spoken of these things to Mary and his children, or perhaps to his friends in the little town where "Joseph's boy" grew up, but none of these words has been recorded or noted or passed on to us.

It is not too difficult though, at least for some of us who are fathers, to imagine certain moments: the long journey to Bethlehem, the scramble to find a place to stay for a wife who is about to give birth with the town full of tourists

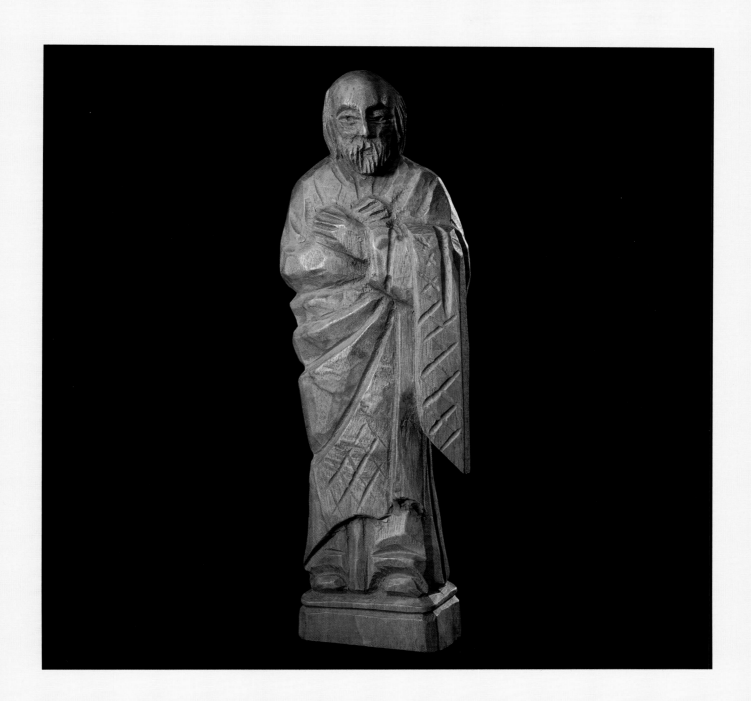

and they were sore afraid.

and the reservations gone awry. The wonder of a birth is always something to behold, even without angels and shepherds and a star hanging overhead.

And we can easily imagine Joseph thinking the things that all fathers think when they first see a little one being born. Even though this Child was to be different, Joseph himself was likely not so different that night from all of us tongue-tied ones, we who stand off to the side or down the hall, extraneous to the moment that belongs to this astonishing thing taking place in the other room. Thinking about how the child will look and whether or not it will be strong. Thinking about what it means to be a father and husband. Thinking about the things that are ahead, the joys and the struggles, the questions and the hopes, the good and the bad. Thinking, more so than anything else, that we may well not be up to the task now that the moment is here, now that the child has come, now that the reality of the dream has begun in earnest.

Some fathers hand out cigars at such a moment, some make dozens of telephone calls, some cheer and laugh and weep. Some, like Joseph perhaps, find that silence is the only response they can muster—and a wondrous silence it is.

It is his silence that still speaks to us all.

And the *angel said unto them, Fear not:*

THIS MARY too is still a mystery, even millions of statues, songs, poems, and prayers later.

This young girl from a small town is inexplicably chosen by God for an astonishing task, as though being a mother is not an astonishing thing on its own. In the moment in which she stands at the threshold of being what all young women dream of being in her day, an angel suddenly confronts her with the message that in some way she will become the mother of us all.

In the moment when she has begun to see herself as a young wife who, she hopes, will also become a young mother someday, she is chosen to carry not only her own hopes and dreams but the hopes and dreams of all people.

for, behold, I bring you good tidings of great joy,

In the moment when she is about to embark on the life that she has always seen herself living, she is asked to forsake that life to live another, more complicated life, complicated in ways that she cannot imagine. One of the mysteries that surrounds her still is why she was chosen in the first place. But another is how she said yes.

And her yes in the face of the unknown, her yes to whatever God was asking her to do, her yes to the belief in the One to come and her being the one to birth it, rear it, protect it, and then let it go—it is her yes that rings as clear as a bell to us. Her yes is the most mysterious part of all.

"BLESSED *are they who have not seen, and yet believed,"* the Child says one day when he has grown up and said yes to his own call. And in the days before the Night of the Child, Mary and Joseph would have been among those who had not seen—not yet.

They were among the first to believe that the One who was to come was, in fact, coming. Such a thing takes faith.

For them to believe that this was indeed the Child is a sign of their faith that God's Promise was true, the Promise that they had been told of by their mothers and fathers before them, a sign of their faith in the ways and the stories and the rituals and oblations of the faithful, a sign of their faith in the Story as it was passed on to them in the ways that all of the stories and rituals and practices of faith are passed on.

Their belief that this was the Child is a sign too of their faith that God speaks to us still, in ways that are both clear and mysterious—a sign of their faith in angels and dreams and the things we can hear when we treasure such things in our hearts.

which shall be to all people.

Their belief that this was the Child is a sign of their faith in the notion of being called by God, a sign of their faith in the goodness of God, in the belief that God will protect those who venture forth when they are called. It expresses their faith that God can be trusted somehow, even when what one is called to do seems preposterous and mysterious and unfathomable.

Whatever else the story of the Night of the Child tells or does not tell us about this Mary and this Joseph, it tells us of their faith—faith seen in the silence of Joseph and in the yes of Mary.

And in the end, the story asks us about our own faith as well. It calls us to silence, to search in our hearts for a yes, and it asks us to believe what we hope is true, that the Promise will be kept.

III

Hope

BLESSED BE THE GOD OF ISRAEL!

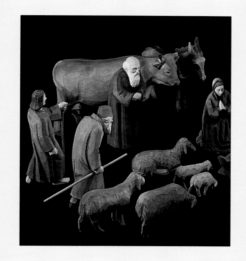

For you have turned to your people and saved them and set them free. You have raised up for us a deliverer from the house of your servant David. And so you promised.

Age after age you proclaimed by the lips of your holy prophets that you would deliver us out of the hands of our enemies, out of the hands of those who hate us.

You have remembered your promise of mercy that you made to our fathers and mothers, and you have remembered the holy covenant that you made with our father Abraham.

And this was the promise that you made: To rescue us and set us free from fear, so that we might worship you with a holy worship, in your holy presence our whole life long.

Benedictus : The Song of Zechariah

THE GOSPEL ACCORDING TO LUKE (AP)

For unto you is born this day

IT IS NIGHT, and it is dark and quiet on these Judean hills, way out south of the city of Jerusalem, away from its noise and bustle.

Perhaps it is chilly too, out in these hills and hollows, these fields where the dew has set. Your clothes are damp, and a breeze comes through every once in a while, sending a chill through you.

You sit by the fire for a few minutes when you can and sleep a little when it is your turn. You chat a little about this or that with the ones who are with you, but mostly you just sit in the dark and listen to the sounds of the night, sounds that have gone on like this forever it seems and will likely go on another forever or two as well.

It is quiet in these hills, though admittedly it is quiet in Bethlehem as well, the little town down below. It is quiet everywhere in such a place, the kind of quiet that one finds in all rural places in the night.

There is the sound of crickets and night birds and raccoons and the others that move in the dark, and perhaps the sound of a branch falling here or there.

There is the sound of water in a creek nearby and the occasional loud crash of something, always startling in the dark, a boulder that has finally moved or a tree that has finally collapsed or a hunting animal that has finally fallen upon its prey. There is the wind in the leaves and in the grass.

All of these sounds become part of, even make up in a way, the silence on these hills in the night. Most nights here, night after night after night, are just this quiet, just this dark, just this ordinary and uneventful.

If you are a shepherd in these hills in the dark of this night, watching your flocks and trying to pass the night in peace and waiting for the dawn, things are the same as they were the night before this one, and the way they will be on the night after this one, and things are as they should be.

Far off to the east, where the sun comes up every morning to take away the darkness, to waken the people who live in these hills, and to give light for the things that take away this silence, it is dark too.

in the city of David a Saviour,

which is Christ the Lord.

In our day and culture, most of us do not see the darkness in the sky in the way that *everyone* did then, not just the shepherds in the fields. The lights of our cities and towns have taken that kind of darkness away from us. To see such darkness now, we generally have to go far away from home. To see such darkness now often requires a drive to the country, a long journey to the shore or to the wilds of Montana, or a safari of sorts to some vast space in Asia or Africa or Latin America, to some space where the machines we have made to chase away the darkness have not yet penetrated. The light that we have manufactured with our machines chases away the darkness to be sure, but it

And this shall be a sign unto you;

also chases away the stars in the heavens and obscures the clouds that are lit up by the moon sometimes. It chases away the tranquility of the twilight and the mystery of the dawn as well. And who knows what is lost along with them.

But here in Judea on this night and there in the east from whence the sun will come, it is a night for watching the heavens, a night where there is enough darkness to see light, whenever it comes, whatever it might mean.

ON THIS NIGHT, according to the story that we are told, two groups of people—the shepherds and the wise men—are watching the heavens. They are watching the heavens for different reasons, in different places, and in different ways, but they are watching nonetheless. If others were watching that night, and we suspect there were, we are not told of them.

These two sets of people see something in that sky that changes everything for them and for all of us for all time. The brief bits of story about these two groups of heaven-watchers tell us very little really. To hear their story, to find it between the lines of the little bit of story given to us in the Gospels, requires a lot of imagining and wondering, the sort of wondering that is probably best done in the dark and the silence while awaiting the arrival of the Light.

THE SHEPHERDS, we are told, are simply minding their own business, which is to say, that they are minding the business of a flock of sheep that may well have belonged to someone else. Shepherds did not own much in those days—or in these days either for that matter. It was, and is, a simple life in many ways.

Ye shall find the babe wrapped in

swaddling clothes,

There is no reason to imagine that these shepherds differed much from any other shepherds or from any other members of the working class in those days. They were not likely literate or if so, just barely. They worked very hard in a poorly regarded job that was hot and dirty and lonely and hard, except for when it was cold and dirty and lonely and hard.

It is hard to imagine that they were well-versed in the Torah or the prophecies or the learned theological discussions of the day. A crowd of men who do such work is not likely to have been big on social graces or to have been traveling in society circles or to have lived in the best part of town. One wonders if the general reaction of townsfolk to seeing the arrival of a crowd of shepherds might not have been something less than joy.

But it is not too hard to imagine them sitting in those hills on that night. Some of them, of course, are half asleep, some of them are sitting in a circle talking the way that people do when they cannot or should not close their eyes and rest.

They are laughing at a story that someone tells or are teasing a young one, a rookie perhaps, about some dumb thing that happened earlier in the day. They are complaining about the food and the weather and about not being home as much as they'd like. Somebody's kid is in trouble, somebody is about to be a father, and somebody just buried his father and his mother is not doing well either. Someone came from Galilee to make his fortune, but it turned out his fortune was not so good, and he ended up here on this hillside tending someone else's sheep. And in between stories, they watch the sky.

They talk of the ordinary stuff of life, and if anyone, anywhere is watching the sky for some momentous event, it is not these men. They are hoping for a quiet night and peace at the last, as the old prayer goes, and for the sheep to behave and for the wolves to stay away and for the rain to hold off and for there to be a decent wage and a decent meal at the end of the week.

They are probably not hoping for angels.

lying in a manger.

UNDERNEATH this same sky, in the east, there were men, so the story tells us, who also watched the heavens. But they were not watching them so casually. These men watched the skies and read the stars and studied the ancient texts, looking for clues as to what might happen next in their world. We do not know exactly where they came from. Was it Persia or Babylon or some other exotic place? So we do not know how far Bethlehem was from the roofs of their houses where they watched the skies, but it was long way from the hills where the shepherds were.

These were men of books, texts, and learning, men of education, philosophy, and letters. They were astronomers, perhaps, or astrologers, men of science, theology, or politics. They were seekers and searchers after the truth of the world. They were the sort of men to whom the halls of power were not fearful nor were they kept closed.

Whatever else they believed in—and we are not told if they were necessarily religious men—they believed in the heavens and the things that the heavens could foretell. They saw something on this night that made them pack up their things and head off in the direction of Jerusalem to see what they could find and to ask questions to get to the bottom of it. Something they saw in that darkness sent them off in search of the king of the Jews.

And without really knowing it, they set off in the direction of the shepherds, the hills, and the little town of Bethlehem.

WHAT HAPPENS next in the story to the shepherds is the stuff of fantasy and legend and myth, which is not to say that it did not take place as

And suddenly *there was with the*

we are told. It is merely to say that even now, after two thousand years of telling the story over and over again to one another and to ourselves, we can hardly imagine it or see it or believe it. We simply do not see such things very often, if at all, so we find it hard to read the story or hear it told and somehow wrap our minds and hearts around it.

No matter how many times we hear it or repeat it to our children or sing it in our songs, it is still a hard thing to grasp, is it not? But the story holds us still, holds us suspended somewhere between disbelief and faith, between doubt and certainty, between fear and hope. That is where the shepherds must have found themselves when the world they knew was suddenly and without warning changed forever in a single night.

An angel appears to them out of the darkness and the silence. Did the angel come strolling out of the darkness, carrying a torch to light the way? Or suddenly appear in the circle around the fire? Did they suspect the angel was a traveler or did they ask for proof?

Suddenly the glory of the Lord surrounds them, which is the only way the glory of the Lord has ever surrounded anyone, when we think about it. There is a glory of the Lord that is always with us—in the sky, the trees, the rain, the laughter of our children, and the warmth of our loved ones. But that is a quiet glory, a glory so profound and encompassing that we have to take care to notice it and be grateful for it each day. But this glory of the Lord, on this night, was different evidently.

The next line of the tale goes through our heads automatically, we who have heard the story so many times—*and they were sore afraid.* They were terrified, scared out of their wits, shaken to their core, and paralyzed with fear. And who would not have been.

The glory of the Lord—this suddenly appearing, completely surrounding sort of glory of the Lord—makes a few appearances over the course of the Story. The one that most readily comes to mind is its brush with Moses.

praising God, and saying,

Whatever it means for the glory of the Lord to surround someone, it was bright enough that the Israelites assigned Moses a tent because the reflection alone was too much for them to bear.

How to describe it: Was it lightning or comets? Was it the star itself hanging down so close to the earth that it lit up the sky? Was it the sort of glowing light that hangs down over the earth the way that cinematographers imagine?

Did it last for seconds or for minutes or for hours? Was it only noticed by the shepherds, or did the whole town wake up? Did the birds awaken and scatter the way they do before a storm? Did the animals in the field head for cover or burrow down deeper? Did the shepherds on the next hill see it too and head for home before it could reach them?

The angel who appeared remains a mystery, as does the heavenly host that appeared soon after. Did they too come strolling across the fields in the dark, singing songs and clapping their hands? Did they swoop down from heaven on the wing? Did they suddenly materialize out of thin air and then disappear the same way?

Fear not, says the angel, though we suspect it took more than the one sentence actually to calm anyone. Those words seem to have settled them, at least from what the narrative tells us. But we find it hard to believe that such a thing was easily done—calming down a crowd after such an experience.

I bring you good news of great joy, says the angel, who then proceeds to announce the arrival of God among us. *Go to the town of David, and look for this sign: a baby wrapped in swaddling clothes and lying in a manger. That is your Savior, Christ the Lord.*

Then more angels appear, however the angels appeared that night, singing and praising God. *Glory to God in the highest*, they sang and shouted. *Peace on earth, and goodwill to all men and women*, they cry.

And then they are gone. Which leaves us there with the shepherds again, on ground that we can more easily imagine. Now we can at least say

Glory to God in the highest,

and on earth peace, good will toward [all].

to ourselves, as some of the shepherds must have done, "Should we head for Bethlehem and see if this is true?"

We can imagine ourselves taking care of all the details that people must tend to in such moments, or at least we think that we can. Someone has to decide who will stay and watch the sheep and who will go back to the house and tell everyone where the rest went. Someone has to figure out who is going to stay with the one who has to stay with the sheep, because no one wants to be left out here alone tonight after what we have all just seen.

We can see ourselves as the ones who instantly believe the angels' strange tale, and we also can see ourselves as those who are not so sure or as those who think that it is all malarkey and would just as soon stay and tend the sheep. We know the one who keeps saying, "What if something happens while we are gone" and the one who keeps saying that we had better hurry before it is too late.

We can see ourselves heading toward town in the dark or even in the dawn, half running, half walking, doing our best to keep up with the rest. And all the time we wonder in our hearts if anything about this night is true or if it is all some crazy dream that seems to have gotten inside our several heads at once and will not let us go. We go hoping that it is true, that we heard correctly, and that we will find the baby in the manger. Yet we set out fearing that we are mistaken somehow, that it is all a joke, or that even if it is true, we will arrive only to find ourselves excluded as shepherds often are.

We can see ourselves on the outskirts of the town, checking all the stables on the streets that we pass. And we see ourselves trying not to get separated from the others, trying to be first to discover what we hope is the place. We see ourselves rounding the corner to hear one of us calling to the others, "In here, in here."

Suddenly what the angels had told us in the dark and the silence in the hills lies enfleshed before us in the manger. What we hoped was true is before us.

And it came to pass,

MEANWHILE on this night, the wise men have been checking their charts and perusing their prophecies and studying their scriptures. No one knows, of course, how long they have been doing such or even how they came to believe that the appearance of this particular star signaled that some extraordinary thing was about to take place.

What we are told is that soon they are packing their bags and heading toward Jerusalem. They seek the star, or at least that is what they say to themselves and to those along the way who ask. They have seen it in the night, and something about the star has made them think that something wondrous is happening. They have to know what it is and what it means.

We have no way of knowing how long their journey was, how many miles or how many days or weeks or months, or how many folks traveled with them, or how long the caravan was or any of the other things that we would like to know and can only imagine. We can be reasonably certain that they did not arrive in Bethlehem on the same night as the shepherds, but that is about all we can figure out.

We have to wonder: What did they say to those they left behind? What did they say to one another that convinced them to make the journey? And what did they *not* say to one another? What things did they keep in their hearts, too afraid to say? What did they expect to discover at the place to which the star seemed to be leading?

We are told that they head first for Jerusalem. When they arrive, they check in with Herod to ask questions about the Child , creating quite a stir. As the current king of the Jews, Herod is more than a little interested in the notion of a new king arriving on the scene. He calls a meeting with the wise men from the east and with the wise men on his payroll to see if anyone knows exactly what is going on.

Next Herod dispatches the visitors to Bethlehem to find out what has gone on and asks them to report back. The wise men set off for the country with high hopes, for the star they have seen goes before them again, guiding them to the place they have sought. Along with their own hopes, they carry Herod's fears, though they may or may not suspect it at the time.

The journey goes on toward the city of David, three men following a star, looking for a child, and hoping that they have accurately understood the signs they have seen and the prophecies they have read.

They cannot say what they think they will find, except that it will be a child. They cannot imagine what will come next or what they will do once they have seen him. By and large we suspect that if it were us on the journey, we would mostly be hoping to find anything at all, hoping we had not come all of this way only to find that our hopes were misplaced.

THE SHEPHERDS by now have been and gone. They came crashing into town on the Night of the Child, excited and noisy, we presume, telling tales of angels, great light, and heavenly hosts.

We do not know about the welcome upon their arrival, or even if anyone in town had noticed. But it is hard to imagine they just slipped in and out of town without shaking up the locals. Folks who are convinced that they have been out in the hills singing with angels are not often shy and retiring.

Indeed, we are told that once the shepherds saw the Child, they spread the word about what they had seen and heard, and that all who heard were amazed at the things they said. And no one, stranger or native, ever goes in and out of a little town without someone's noticing and telling the tale, adding a little bit to flesh in the story if need be.

into heaven,

We can easily imagine little crowds at the coffee shop at the corner, listening to the story, asking questions, offering theories, inquiring as to which stable it was and who these people were anyway.

We can imagine the arrival of the local clergy, eager to see if the tale were true and acceptable and if it meant that the character of the stories they told about the ways of God had changed.

We can see scholars, scribes, and thinkers scrambling back through their scriptures, trying to make this story make sense. We can see doubters and disbelievers as well, those who have been fooled before, or at least they thought so, and are wary of being fooled again.

Probably the shepherds and wise men were not the only people who visited, nor were wise men the only ones who read the prophecies. These are simply the only stories that we are given. As bare as the facts are, it is within them that we must seek the truth.

AND THEN they arrive at the place where the Child is to be found, these shepherds and these wise men.

It is not much of a place, according to the story, not the sort of place one would expect to find such a Child, a Child heralded by angels, sought by wise men, foretold by prophets, and longed for by a nation.

Who can believe that this is the place and that this is the time and that this is the One?

The story of the shepherds tells us nothing about what they do or say, only that they are amazed that they have actually found what the angels have told them that they will find. And because that much is true, they believe everything else they have been told about this Child as well. And whatever all of those things are, they are enough to send them through the countryside

Let us now go

even unto Bethlehem,

telling everyone what they have seen and heard—or at least as much of it as they understand.

The wise men take a different tack. They come prepared to worship the Child, which they do, we are told, with what must have been a certain amount of perplexity at the arrival of the Child into such a place.

They offer gifts of the treasures they have brought along on the journey: gold, frankincense, and myrrh. Such offerings must seem strange to the young mother and her husband. Somehow these strangers know some of what Mary and Joseph know.

People are coming and going by now. The shepherds have come and gone, telling their story and no doubt urging people to go and see for themselves. The wise men have attracted no small amount of attention in this little town with its crowd of tourists left over from the census. Word has begun to spread, and others will be headed to Bethlehem to see this this thing that has come to pass.

And in the midst of all are the mother and Child, this mother who treasures these things, holding them in her heart, turning them over and over again in hope, wonder, and astonishment, this Child who has come to be God among us.

SOON IT will be our turn once more.

Each year we tell the story of the Night of the Child. The story has become an unavoidable part of our culture's fabric, for good and for not so good sometimes, in a way that makes it all but impossible to ignore—or at least its telling.

To be sure, we need not believe the story to call it into our consciousness at the end of each year. The buyers and the sellers, the devoted and the doubtful, the uncertain and the unfaithful—all of us tell the story, or at least we tell *of* the story. The story is never far from any of us as the year winds down into the winter months. That is neither good nor bad, simply the case in the time and the place where most of us live.

We wonder from time to time what it would be like to hear the story for the first time, again, now that we are older and perhaps even wiser, when the story might confront us with its mystery, power, and astonishing news. Perhaps now we might be forced to choose whether to believe it or not.

We have heard the story so many times and in so many ways that it has become almost powerless, in a way, stripped of wonder and amazement. The characters are so familiar to us—mother, baby, father, shepherds, angels, wise men, and all the rest—that we can hardly even hear them or see them, even in our imaginations. We have become so familiar with the story they collectively tell that we can hear nothing new in it at all.

All too often nothing in the story cries out to us or astonishes us. Nothing frightens, mystifies, amazes us, or makes us sore afraid. Nothing sends us off to follow a star or to sing a song or to run to see this thing that has come to pass.

Our familiarity with the story has bred in us, if not contempt, as the sage might have said, then at least some measure of indifference or lassitude or disregard. We are too sophisticated, too wise, too well-informed to believe it as wholeheartedly as we might. It is little wonder then, that we hear it each year with so little wonder in our heart and then find that it has so little power to move us or to change us or to shape us into something other than casual observers of a long-told story that we can hardly believe.

IT IS NOT so hard to believe that none of those people was sure about very many things at all that night, anymore than we are each year, even as we head down the calendar of days toward the one we celebrate as the Night of the Child.

If you are Mary and hear the news she heard, how can you believe that it could possibly be true? You are not even married yet and have only had a young girl's notions of what it will mean to have a child, much less any notion of what it might mean to have the Child.

If you are Joseph and the dream comes to you, how can you even begin to believe that these things are true about the young woman you are about to marry and the child you are about to raise?

If you are one of the shepherds awakened by the angels proclaiming a Savior's birth and you can go and see for yourself, how can you be anything but skeptical and afraid and uncertain of what you have heard?

If you are a wise man, how can you journey off to a far country, following a star that may be no more than just that, and keep a straight face when fellow travelers ask you where you are going and what you are seeking?

And, if you are one of us, people like you and like me, at the beginning of the third thousand years in which this story is told, and you can see for yourself all the trouble and darkness and clamor that the world still holds after two thousand years of telling this story, how can you believe that the story is true? How can you repeat it again and again, and not wonder if you are only dreaming or wishing? How can you be sure that you are not only hoping that the story is true but wanting it to be so?

What we fear, of course, is that the story is not true, that somehow, somewhere it has been garbled in the telling or it was misunderstood from the start. The story's sheer preposterousness is a little hard for us to get over, whether we are willing to say that aloud to anyone, or even to ourselves. Angels, dreams, virgin births, wise men, stars, and such are not the stuff of conversation in our time, at least not acceptable conversation most of the time, we would rather not admit that much of our faith is based in such a wild and wondrous tale.

Perhaps we would have an easier time if we possessed more extensive documentation, if someone had made better notes from which to write up the Gospel accounts. Some video footage would have been nice as well. The story requires far more faith in things unseen than we children of the scientific age feel comfortable with, there are too many holes in the story and too many unanswered questions.

We may be tempted to write the whole thing off as pure myth and metaphor, to dismiss out of hand the things that we cannot touch with our hands. Such a temptation comes to all of us at one time or another, in some Advent season or another, even to the most devout among us. Perhaps that is why we tell the story over and over again.

Some years when we hear the story, we are convinced that it is true. Sometimes when we hear the story, we cannot believe it. And most years we

live somewhere in between, hoping against hope that the story is worth believing at all, hoping against hope that we can believe it.

We believe it, and we pray to be helped with our unbelief.

THE ANNUAL telling of the story of the Night of the Child always seems to take us back, back to our own childhoods, back to our families, back to the children who have been in our lives—the sons and daughters, nieces and nephews. Telling the story is the one event of the year that seems to take us back most powerfully.

and found Mary and Joseph,

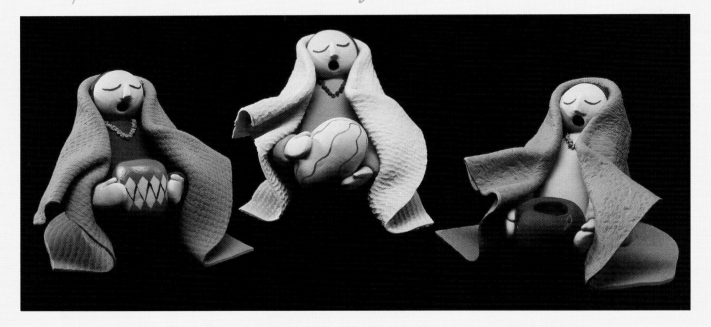

and the babe lying in a manger.

The telling does so partly because it reminds us of the places where we first heard the story and of the people who told it to us.

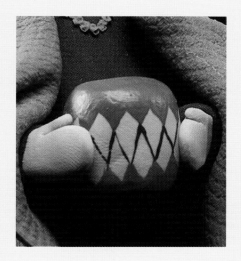

We remember our first Christmas pageant with the grown-ups dressed as shepherds and wise men and Mary and Joseph and the angels. We remember the wild collection of bathrobes, halos, and fake beards, and we remember the way we all stared down into the manger at the newborn child who had been pressed into service to act the part of the baby Jesus, and we wondered if this is what the baby Jesus actually looked like.

We are taken back to a living room in an old house that everyone we know has moved away from now and to our place on the floor beside our grandfather's big chair or to our place in our mother's lap on the couch by the window. We can hear our grandfather reading the story in that voice we loved so well but can now hardly recall, except at certain moments when this story is read again in our hearing. Our cousins are there and the candles are glowing and the fire crackles and there are tears in our father's eyes when we catch him looking at us across the room.

We recall the afternoons spent unpacking the crèche and setting it up in the window seat under the big bay window in the living room. We built the stable out of stones and pieces of wood that we found in the yard, and we brought sand in to spread around because somewhere in our heads we had an idea that Bethlehem was in the desert. Straw was spread around the manger itself, and each character in the story was placed with care at what must have been just the right place. And on the mantel we put the baby in a little box from which he will not be released until after Christmas Eve dinner.

Our memory takes us back to that night we drove to the park in the center of town, the park where they always have the big art festivals and the big band concerts. At Christmas they had the big crèche too, the one we rolled down the car windows to see, and we felt the cold air blow in and sting our faces. Angels were hung in the trees, and a giant electric star hung down over the manger.

And when they had seen it,

There were real sheep there that night and real donkeys and real cows and real people in the stable. And a real long line of people were trying to get close enough to see it all firsthand and even to touch it. We stood in the cold and waited our turn and wondered if there were any children at the stable that night so long ago.

We remember the days when we acted out the Christmas story at the top of the stairs in the hallway, the annual event when we dressed up and played all the parts and memorized all the lines. Our grandparents and parents sat in chairs at the bottom of the stage and laughed and cried as we told the story. They talked about us in whispered tones when we disappeared offstage to change costumes and to search for more and better props. This was the play we spent all Christmas afternoon rehearsing and planning because it was the last thing that everyone did together before grandfather went off to play the organ at midnight mass.

We can somehow remember, as though there were any chance we could forget, that year when the telling of the story first fell to us. And we remember who was missing from the table that first time and how much we missed them and how uncertain we were that we could step into those shoes to and pass on this story and all that it had come to mean to us and to those whom we love.

We recall the Christmas Eve nights that were supposed to be nights of celebration and somehow became something else. Nights when anger, fear, and brokenness found their way into our homes and our living rooms and sat down alongside us at the table, nights when the news we had just heard was almost too much to bear. We remember the nights when someone who was to come and share this table and this story had chosen once again not to come, and the place that had been set would be empty instead, nights when we experienced no peace at our table and so not much peace on earth, as far as we were concerned. Nights when there was not enough joy to get through supper, much less to spread round the world.

There were nights too when the rumors of war had become more than just rumor, and we sat down to tell the story of the Child knowing that somewhere bombs were being dropped on children by children of our own. And we knew that the angels would be busy that evening, and we hoped they would bring peace on earth or at least usher in a cessation of hostilities.

We recall too the Christmas Eve mass when we first understood the connection between this story of the Child and the story of the Cross. On that night we celebrated his birth by kneeling at his table, the place where we first realized that this Child of God had somehow made it possible for us to become the children of God as well.

We remember that night and the way the candles seemed more brilliant than they ever have before or have been since. And the sudden burst of light when the vestments and cloths on the pulpit and altar were turned over to symbolize the arrival of the Light of the world. And our sudden astonishing realization that we believed the whole thing was true, maybe for the first time, and from that moment forward nothing in our lives would ever be the same again.

told them concerning this child.

On that night hundreds of us gathered in the sanctuary, holding candles, singing songs, and parading out the back door singing joy to the world. How amazing the faces all looked when we turned around and saw them lit up, heads thrown back in song and smiles shining through. That night when we walked out the church door into the street and wanted to walk all the way home in this parade, through the streets of the city, shouting the song at the top of our lungs.

We remember the night we sat outside in the country all Christmas Eve in the dark by a fire, the cold wrapped around us, and the snow flashed by against the firelight. The sounds of livestock down in the fields below and the light of the stars after the snow shower had gone. We wondered if this was what it is like to be one of the shepherds, and if we might sit here long enough to be surrounded by the glory of God. And then, the sudden realization that we were, we are in fact, if we only could believe it.

And all they that heard it

wondered at those things

AND NOW here we all are again, the whole motley crowd of us, all gathering up to tell and to hear and to celebrate the story once again. We are all the same too, except for the places where we are different, both different from who we were last year, and different from each other.

For some of us, it has been a fine year, this one that has passed since we last sat down to await the telling of the story of the Night of the Child. Some of our dreams have come true and some of our questions have been answered and some of our problems have been solved and some of our needs have been met.

We have found good work to do or finished some good thing off in fine fashion and have even had a chance to catch our breath. Some of us have moved and found a new place that is becoming home more quickly than we thought it might, and discovered new people with whom to share our journeys and days and lives, new people who have made our lives richer and fuller and more than we thought they could ever be.

We have had our share of ups and downs, but there have been ups mostly, and the downs have not seemed to be more than we could handle. And no one has showed up to tell us that the ups were a mistake somehow and that we were going to have to turn the good stuff back in as soon as the weekend was over.

For some of us though, our year's journey has been harder than we could have dreamed that it would be or could be. Someone will not be here to share the trip toward Bethlehem with us this year, and we cannot imagine going without them. Some of us are carrying a burden that we cannot seem to shake and are uncertain how much longer we can bear it.

Some of us are not well in mind, body, or estate, as the prayer book says, and our futures, with or without the journey to Bethlehem, are more than a little uncertain. Some of us have lost much in the last year, much more than we gained. And though we are far enough along on the journey to know that life can always be counted on to lead us through hard places sometimes, it seems that this year we have seen more than our fair share.

Some of us are poor and lonely and lost and afraid. Some of us are in prison or in the hospital. Some of us are dying and some of us are trapped in violent places where war and hatred and brutality are the norm rather than the exception.

Some of us have spent the year fighting for justice and peace and have a sense that we have hardly made a dent. Some of us have spent our days, hours, strength, and spirit caring for children or the sick or the elderly, and we are worn down by the sheer dailiness of it. We are worn too by the knowledge that sometimes all we can do is not enough to make the difference we had hoped to make.

Some of us are being left out still because of color or race or some other thing that should be celebrated rather than cursed. Some of us have been left behind without resources or opportunity, with little chance of having either one in the near future.

But Mary kept all these things,

Some of us live lives of gracious plenty and others live lives of desperate need. Some of us wield power and some of us are oppressed. Some of us are confident about the future, whatever it may bring. Some of us are afraid of the coming evening and none too certain what daylight will bring, or if we will even see it.

Some of us have much and cannot bear to look at ourselves in the mirror some days, others of us consider ourselves blessed and smile like we know it, even though we do not own a mirror to look in.

Everything is the same, and everything is different, just as it has been for all time, just as it was on the night two thousand years ago. From Nazareth to Jerusalem to Bethlehem to the East, wherever that was, things were the same as they are now. It was quieter and it was darker on those streets and in those hills in that time long ago, but we were all there then, just as we are now.

Some of us are waiting to see what will come of the prophet's words, some to see if the time will pass quietly, some are watching the heavens and looking for the Light. Some of us are waiting to see if what the angels say is true, some to see if we have understood our own dreams at all. Some of us are waiting to see if the world will be any different in the morning, some to see if morning actually will come.

"The story of any one of us," Frederick Buechner pointed out once, "is the story of us all." If he is right, and one suspects he is, then we were all there then, and we will all soon be there again, carrying the hopes and fears of all the years.

There will be for us in Bethlehem, in the city of David, a Savior to be born. And we will choose between our hope and our fear.

THE NIGHT of the Child is the night of hope, all hopes. We await the coming of this Night with all our hopes bound up together somehow, both our hopes for ourselves as individuals and our hopes for others as well, both those who are known to us and those who are unknown.

We await this Night hoping that if confronted by angels, we can say yes, that our faith will be strong enough and sturdy enough not to shrink toward what is comfortable and away from what can make straight the paths of the Lord and prepare the way for the coming of the Christ.

We wait in the hope that when the moment comes, we will, like the shepherds, have the presence of mind to hear the heavenly host and the spirit to head off to Bethlehem to see this thing which has come to pass. We hope that we will find the Child and be found by the Child too, and that we will find ourselves full of wonder and amazement and joy and praise. And that we will return to our places telling everyone what we have seen and heard, bearing witness at least to our own astonishment.

There is a hope in us that we too might be willing to travel far, armed like the wise men with the ancient scriptures and the old stories, and believe that the star will lead us. And that we will have faith that the star will guide us to the place where we will see the Child, and that we too can offer our gifts and our worship, that we will be moved to do so in an instant.

And we hope there will be things to treasure in our hearts, things to ponder, hold, and remember, and that we will be thoughtful enough to see those things and wise enough to hold onto them.

We hope that it will be as the angels have said: that we will come to pay homage at the stable, and the Child will be there for us again—or for the first time maybe. That on this Night we can hope for peace on earth and goodwill to all people. That on this Night we shall see the beginning of the end of the things that divide us, that this Night's celebration and remembrance will be remembered as a turning point in the story of us all.

We hope too that we can believe the story with all our hearts and with all our minds and with all our strength and with all of any other part of us that we

And the shepherds returned,

can bring to bear. That we can see our own sweet selves in this story and know deep within in us that it is our story too.

And we hope that we can see the face of God in the story as well, in the faces of the shepherds, in the faces of Mary and Joseph, in the face of the Child.

WE CARRY IN US the hope that we can tell the story to our children, that we can tell it with conviction and passion and spirit and wonder—that the story will still live in us, even though we do not understand it at all in some ways and understand it too well in others. That we can teach it to them with the same reverence and joy with which it has been given to us. That we can somehow pass on some of what this all means to us.

We hope that our retelling this year will come someday to hold a cherished place in our memories, that somewhere in the hustle and the noise of the season itself, a moment of joy and wonder will break in upon us and within us and around us. And that we will have the presence of mind to be present to the moment, to hold it and to ponder it and treasure it in our hearts.

MORE THAN anything else, of course, we hope that the telling of the story will change us—for good if not forever, for a while if not for all time.

We hope and pray that our lives will be renewed by the birth of this Child. We hope that our darkness will be brightened by the coming of the Light of the world.

We hope that the Prince of Peace will bring us exactly that, for ourselves, for those we love, for all of us. We hope that the world will not be the same when the daylight comes upon us.

glorifying and praising God

We hope that we will come face-to-face with the glory of God and that we will be sore afraid, and that we will rejoice, joining our voices with the angels and archangels who forever sing songs of praise and worship.

We hope the story is all true, for all time, for all of us. And we hope that we have the courage to believe it.

AND NOW it is time once again.

It is time again for traveling each to our own city to be counted and greeted and held for a while, time to sing a hosanna or two around midnight, the one song worth singing when songs are to be sung. It is time to be wakened by angels and to run through the countryside seeking a Child.

It is time for us to leave our flocks and our fields and our farms unattended, while we search for the One we have not seen in a while. It is time to follow the star in the East and to bear gifts and perhaps to outwit the king by going home by new paths.

It is time to be still and to listen for the one Voice worth hearing where voices are heard. *Let there be light,* it once whispered. *And they will know Me by My name, and I will come to them,* it once said. More softly now it says, *It is time, it is time once again.*

It is time for the Promise once again to be fulfilled in a single night. It is time for the Night of the Child.

IV

Love

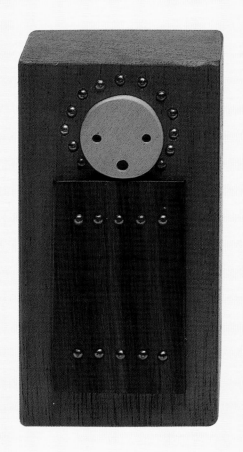

Now, Lord, let your servant depart in peace, as you have promised.

For with my own eyes I have seen the Savior: The One You prepared for all the world to see, the Light to enlighten all the earth, the One Who will bring glory to Your people for evermore.

Nunc dimittus : The Song of Simeon

THE GOSPEL ACCORDING TO LUKE (AP)

IN THE END, ON THIS NIGHT OF ALL NIGHTS, there will only be a baby in a manger in a stable in a small town in a small country far away. And there will have been a couple of thousand of these nights that have passed. And what the birth of this Child, this baby that lies in the manger, means to us is largely up to us.

Though the Spirit moves where and how it wills and stories abound of powerful moments in the lives of those who somehow really caught a glimpse of the Mystery behind this Child, it is still by and large up to us as to whether this Night will once again speak to us of the Love that is there to be found.

IT WILL BE up to us to prepare our hearts for the Night of the Child, to prepare the way of the Lord, to make straight the paths. It will be up to us to make a journey of sorts toward Bethlehem, to spend some time listening to the story as it weaves its way through Advent. We are the ones who must make room in our hearts for the story to speak, who must listen carefully to its twists and its turns, listening for the places where it begins to tell us our own story.

The season will be full of stories, of family and friends, of Christmases long ago, of memories and hopes and half-forgotten days gone by. And in the midst of them, we must take care that we do not neglect the telling of the story. We must be present to its telling, if we hope for it to touch our hearts. We are the ones who must ponder in our hearts what all of this has to teach us about the Story of us all.

It will be up to us to leave our flocks and our fields unattended for a while. It will fall to us manage our time and our energy and our calendars and our schedules. We are the ones who must make sure that there is a place and the time to be silent and thoughtful, to rest and contemplate. We are the ones who must seek out the time to prepare our hearts and minds for the coming of the Night of the Child.

for all the things that they had heard and seen,

EACH YEAR we tell ourselves that we tried to do too much at the holidays, each year we realize that we were so busy with Christmas that we missed the Child. Most of the time we have only ourselves to blame, of course. The Child will come. Will we be there? is the question.

It will be up to us to follow the star when we see it. We are the ones who must somehow summon the courage to believe in its Light and to follow wherever it leads. We are the ones who must head off to a place that is unknown to us still after all of these years, and hope and believe that what we seek will be found there.

It will be up to us to say yes to the angels when they are among us. It will fall to us to join in their songs and to take their advice and head off to the stable to see this thing which has come to pass.

We must be willing to listen for the Voice in the voices of those around us, to suspend our disbelief if only for a little while, to listen for the question being asked of us in this season and by this season. If we would see the Child on this Night, we too must be willing to dream and to hope and to believe.

If we would see the Child on this Night, then we must be prepared perhaps even to be a child on this Night, to let our imagination and our hope and our faith carry us to some new way of seeing, some new way of hearing, so that our eyes might be opened and our ears might be too, so that our hearts might be quickened and our spirits might be touched.

In the end, we must be willing to believe in the Promise that Immanuel will come, we must have faith to believe that the Promise will be kept, and we must hope that we too will be willing and able and childlike enough to recognize the face of God in the face of the Child.

A WISE MAN—not one of those wise men, but a wise man nonetheless—once said that he was certain only that these three things were true: that God is Love, that somehow that Love got loose on earth in the person of Jesus Christ, and that if one believed those two things, then everything could never be the same again.

What might happen to us and within us and among us if we were indeed to prepare our hearts and follow the star and leave our flocks and our fields and make haste to Bethlehem to see this thing which has come to pass? What might we see and what might we hear and what might we come to believe that would change everything for us forever?

WE MIGHT begin to believe that the Light will indeed shine in the darkness and that the darkness will never overcome it. We might begin to know in our hearts that no darkness that we find ourselves in is too dark for us after all, that the One who made us will come searching for us again and again, choosing to come and be among us, choosing to share in that darkness and to burst it apart with light and life and hope and love.

We might begin to believe that we indeed have seen the thing that many prophets and wise ones and not so wise ones had longed to see but could not see, had longed to hear but could not hear, that God is with us, in a child, in a person, in a Savior.

We might begin to believe that the glory of the Lord does still shine indeed, surrounding us all from time to time, leaving us breathless and wondering, leaving us sore afraid and mightily joyous. That we too can be bathed in that Light and that we too can join our voices with the angels from time to time, praising God in the highest.

We might begin to believe that peace on earth may yet be possible, even if only in bits and pieces in this corner and in that one, in this home and in that one—ours too even. We might begin to believe that goodwill to all is the only proper response to such news and begin to offer it even as we return to our own homes telling the amazing story to those whom we pass along the way.

We might begin to believe that indeed love has gotten loose on earth somehow—not just any love but the one true Love—the Love that has the power to change us all, the Love that has brought us into being and has now brought Love itself into being in the person of this baby in a manger.

We might begin to believe that the sharing in and the sharing of that Love, however and wherever we can, in ways great and small, is the only thing worth doing while we are here. And that all of our lives must be ordered around that one true necessity.

We might even begin to believe that God loves us, each of us and all of us. That no one of us is separated from that Love or ever has been, or ever really will be again.

We might even begin to believe that God loves us not only enough to make promises but to keep them. That if God will keep this one, then perhaps all of them are true and that goes for the promises made to our mothers and fathers and our sons and our daughters and our neighbors.

We might even begin to believe that indeed only love matters at all in this world: God's love for us and our love for God and each other. The proof is to be found in the Love that is lying there in the manger in the stable in the dark of the night, because that Love has been loosed in the world in the the only way we could ever hope to understand it—in a child like us and for us and with us.

BEHOLD, *I am about to do something new. Can you not perceive it?*

It is the question with which we began—or at least one of them. It is the annual question that accompanies the Promise and the story and the Night of the Child itself.

We hope that when all is said and done we can say yes this year, along with Mary and with Joseph.

We hope too that the glory of the Lord shines round about us some too this year, perhaps even enough to make us sore afraid and then to send us off to try to describe it to someone.

We hope that when the angels begin to sing that we join in with as much joy as we can muster.

And we hope that we can find a gift of something dear and something precious to offer in the stable alongside the ones who came seeking the star and found the Child for their trouble.

We hope that when this something new happens again this year that we can indeed perceive it. And that we see it as the fulfillment of the Promise itself.

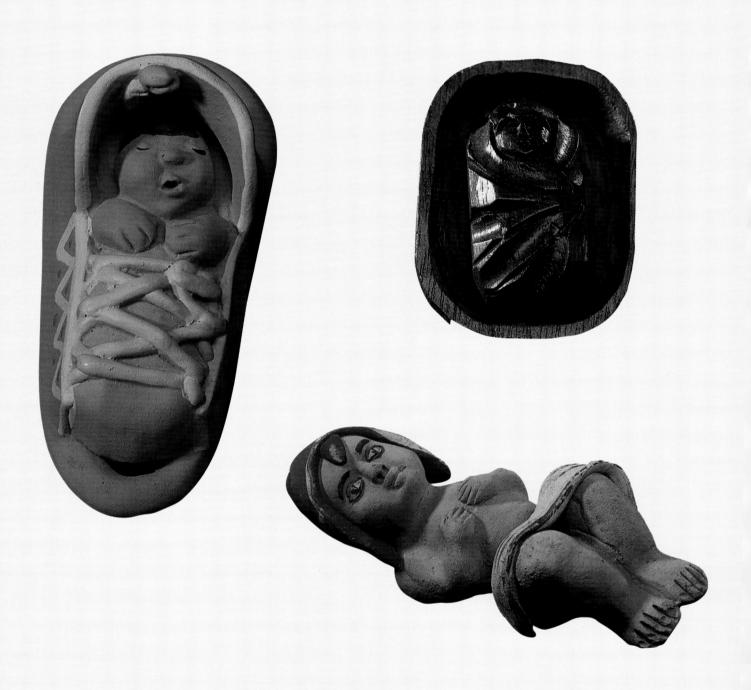

ACKNOWLEDGMENTS

Majolica baptismal bowl. *Pages 2, 3*

United States. "The Spirit of Bethlehem." White bisque porcelain. Used by permission of Boehm Porcelain Studio. *Pages 22, 23, 72, 73, 113*

Switzerland. Carved wood. *Pages 60, 61, 100, 101, 112*

Philippines. Carved acacia wood. *Pages 18, 19, 112*

United States. Tennessee. Corn shuck by Pearl Bowling. *Pages 4, 5, 68, 69*

Nigeria. Yoruba tribe. Carved thorn wood. *Pages 20, 21, 62, 63, 81*

Thailand. Reed and cloth. *Page 7*

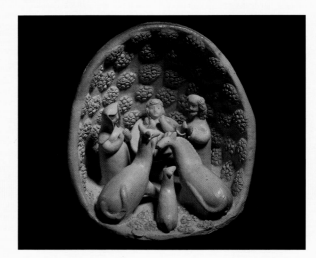

Guatemala. Bisque clay. *Pages 10, 11*

"Adoration of the Magi." Carved wooden plaque.
Pages 78, 79

United States. Tennessee. Carved wood (walnut, cherry,
mahogany, ash). *Pages 36, 37, 112*

Poland. Wood. *Pages 42, 43*

Bolivia. "Head of the Madonna." Carved wood by Ramiro
Valverde. *Pages 40, 41*

Mexico. Painted clay. *Pages 34, 35, 70*

Spain. Painted baked mud. *Pages 96, 97*

Brazil. Painted glazed clay. *Pages 38, 39, 82, 83*

United States. Pewter. Used by permission of Hudson Pewter, Hudson, Mass. *Pages 50, 51, 84, 85, 113*

Germany. Carved wood. *Pages 24, 25*

Peru. "Retablos." *Pages 28, 29*

Czechoslovakia. Paper dolls. *Pages 108, 109*

El Salvador. Painted wooden plate. *Pages 26, 27*

France. "Santons." Painted clay. *Pages 12, 13, 98, 99*

Sri Lanka. Painted wood. *Pages 102, 103*

Zimbabwe. Woven reed with traditional native cloth. *Page 105*

Democratic Republic of the Congo. Carved wood. *Pages 30, 31, 52, 53, 86, 87, 113*

Korea. Carved wood. *Pages 88, 89, 120*

United States. Southwestern Native American. Painted clay. *Pages 90, 91, 120*

Peru. Painted clay. *Pages 55, 120*

United States. New Mexico. Painted clay. Used by permission of JoVenia (Jodi) Jones. *Pages 44, 45, 64, 65, 74, 75, 92, 93, 121*

United States. Carved cedar wood by Leo G. Salazar. Used by permission of Leonardo G. Salazar and Lydia M. Salazar. *Pages 56, 57, 121*

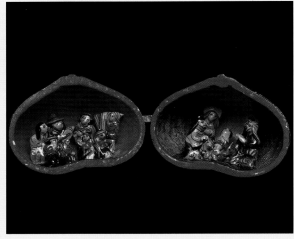

Peru. Gourd. *Pages 106, 107*

Honduras. Dried seed pods. *Pages 94, 95*

Haiti. Carved wood. *Pages 48, 49*

United States. Hawaii. Various natural materials (coconut shell, starfish, bamboo, nuts) and fabric by Jean Judd. *Pages 14, 46*

United States. Stoneware clay. Copyright © 1966 and used by permission of Belinda E. Patterson. Jackson, Tenn. *Pages 76, 77, 121*

United States. Ukrainian egg. Wax-resist technique on duck egg. Used by permission of Cheryl Christensen. *Page 33, cover*

United States. Ukrainian egg. Wax-resist technique on duck egg. Used by permission of Cheryl Christensen. *Page 67, back cover*

ABOUT THE UPPER ROOM

UPPER ROOM MINISTRIES *began in 1935 with the publication of a daily devotional magazine called* The Upper Room, *now published in 70 editions and 44 languages throughout the world. The Upper Room's mission is to encourage people in a vital and transforming relationship with God.*

The Upper Room Museum, established in 1953 and located between Nashville's Music Row and Vanderbilt University, welcomes thousands of visitors each year. The museum houses many items that relate to the life of prayer and devotion in addition to the Nativity Collection represented in this book. The first nativity set for the collection was purchased in 1965. Now, over one hundred nativity sets in The Upper Room Museum collection represent many of the different cultures in which the magazine is published and read. From carved figures and exquisite porcelains to simple field stones they all tell the story of the Night of the Child.